Blade Pitch Control Unit

SEAN BONNEY was born in Brighton, grew up in the north of England, and he now lives in London. He has published a number of pamphlets, and his poems and essays have featured in many of the leading innovative magazines. Known as an exhilarating performer of his work, he has performed in London, Cambridge, Portugal, Prague and New York. A part time lecturer, he has taught at Birkbeck College, Roehampton, and the University of Southampton.

Blade Pitch Control Unit

SEAN BONNEY

SALT

CAMBRIDGE

PUBLISHED BY SALT PUBLISHING
PO Box 937, Great Wilbraham, Cambridge PDO CB1 5JX United Kingdom

© Sean Bonney, 2005

The right of Sean Bonney to be identified as the
author of this work has been asserted by him in accordance
with Section 77 of the Copyright, Designs and Patents Act 1988.

First published 2005

Printed and bound in the United Kingdom by Lightning Source

Typeset in Swift 9.5 / 13

ISBN-10 1 84471 251 6 paperback
ISBN-13 978 1 84471 251 9 paperback

SP

1 3 5 7 9 8 6 4 2

To the memory of
Burhan Tufail
1963–2004

Contents

THE DOMESTIC POEM (2000)

cross harbour . . .   3
walk on. strike softly away from children . . .   4
It doesn't matter if music's attached . . .   5
Fast. Victoria to Warren St   6
Mayday   7
There's got to be something . . .   9
Just going down there to post a letter . . .   10
Certain young aristocrats . . .   11
calling all dogs . . .   12

THE ROSE (2000)

pop stars on Holloway Road   15
For Bob, Cobbing Through the Soundhole, Where Cobbing IS   23

NOTES ON HERESY (2000–2001)

Tom O'Bedlam   27
Defects in the Structure of the State   31
Lyric Poetry: Surveillance   37
Confessional Poetry   45

POISONS, THEIR ANTIDOTES (2001–2003)

The Management Consultant Has Gone for Lunch   55
Paul Verlaine reads poems on Old Compton St   65
Expulsions (on Marchmont St with coffee)   67
Poisons, their Antidotes   71

FILTH SCREED (2003–2004)

all poetry that does not . . .   87
stood . . .   88

ant sore . . .   89

sketch . . .   90

questionable savagery . . .   91

thin suns bleat . . .   92

his opened mouth . . .   93

a lattice of swallow-screech . . .   94

this is a shop spurt yellow gas . . .   95

fly track . . .   96

at 9.38 you hear voices . . .   97

alembic strip neutral . . .   99

enabled history on the ant crawl . . .   100

the details at times are as vague as burn screams . . .   101

silver burst . . .   102

the words "we are loyal employees" . . .   104

I don't . . .   105

86 him . . .   107

'these' pictures have come in lately . . .   108

click . . .   110

glue, magnetized . . .   111

hold on. does the traffic not worry . . .   112

Branson's mouth imposed . . .   113

and he, who want to be adverts . . .   114

this is a love poem in 42cm . . .   115

bone sweat . . .   116

lids flicker . . .   117

the map of London . . .   118

survive commerce on . . .   120

nothing of importance . . .   121

Burnt Nickle (2004–2005)

morally . . .   125

we understand . . .   126

demand protection for sex dolls . . .   127

social climbing among metals . . .   128

that the police station as system . . .   130

consumerism speaks only . . .   131

on cell wall . . .   133

Verdict :   134

Oona King   136

Document (2005)

Filter OD   143

Document   148

Document: No Admittance   150

Document: Suicide Note   152

Acknowledgments

Thanks are due to Jeff Hilson of Canary Woof, Bob Cobbing of Writers Forum, Alan Halsey of West House Books, Keston Sutherland and Andrea Brady of Barque Press, for publishing earlier versions of these poems.

Versions of some of these poems have featured in the following journals : *And, Quid, cul-de-qui, The Gig, CCCP Review 13, Action Poetique, Boxon, Poetry Summit 2004.*

The Domestic Poem (2000)

(cross harbour. at the right. windy crossroad. past the george.
keep to left. got a market on your body. 3 souls. left at school.
1 minute. Manchester road. 3 minutes.

**leg twitch. listen. the forest door. or brewing coffee / the
kitchen table. papers. hissing. waiting (where d'you put
that voice (left at the siren. blowing stones**

walk on. strike softly away from children.
image: 30,000 years. but shops remain.
got open eye hatch life. sea-lilies, sea-whip:
walk on. pearls in fists, turn up to force 8 &
gizza kiss, to crack on these ribs,
go shopping. for tanks for furnace for fibre
for nettle. them homes are taken. built
from nails them homes. strike softly. siren
step stone. step it, his pretty property
ground to pebbles. & spitting. & shopping.
carried in pockets to river. & nettle. & fibre.
& coils. & rain. & shadows rumble . . . . . .

It doesn't matter if music's attached to the scene when **your ears are stuffed with silver**. Each house is on its own cycle, you walk in from the street and the scene changes *what secret is this*. Perhaps the house of someone you've never known. Perhaps a landscape. In the foreground, a sovereign, a child. Placing the head in his wide mouth.

A photo on the wall and sounds glued to the windows. Border sound. Imsonic (and a presence behind the walls. That you know what it is and shadows. Bookbreath. How to get to and eat it. How lipfuck. To get the tongue in (**in other words // what that means // photocopy the dictionary paste it over the windows you'll still see the sky but**

Fast. Victoria to Warren St

got getta
back to my flat
gotta flat gotta key cos gotta flat gotta TV
gotta lovely gotta cat gotta flower got
got gotta come got gotta see
what mirror what left at the mirror
back of my
mirror
gotta lovely pussy cat
& gonna
& gonna
feed him his whiskers
gonna buy him gonna flower gonna go to that
whats that
the name of that   whirlpool
the name of that   jasmine
the name of that   shop
gonna go to that that
whats that name of   which is what
                            which is larger
                            the honey or the padlock
                            the honey or the
got blood got blue river glue powdered blue
got the name of that   shop
sell paper dust and padlock dust dust and
cigarettes   it sells cigarettes
gonna go to that   yeah
gonna go to that   jasmine
that   lovely
gonna buy gonna   cigarettes
get my pussy cat
gonna take him for walkies

Mayday

Whatever's missing will be here by spring.
you can date it, you can wrap it, you can
stamp it flat. Don't you worry, it's instant
product. Don't worry about what it is,
it'll bore us. Here in the market we're eating
dogs and honey. Whatever's missing
has never stopped yelling, it was always
the wax in our ears, was amoeba conduction.
I accord no sympathy, no ginger digression,
but flesh it, and the planet moves. Its
a question of biting the hand, expectant
child vs. real fangs. Its called dehydration,
locked in the square till the chief pig rises
from the soil where dust was thrown. Magma
dust, boiling, scorch alembic, transformed
on the bone track its simply what happens,
its every good kid's duty, to smash up
McDonald's and eat some granite. You know
you could choke for years. Or you could stop it.
With the third stone it's possible to discover any
person in any part of the world: did you hear
about that guy who went to a party with a brick
on his face, as the chirping of birds, the lowing
of beasts. Shame begins the dawn shall become
a true oracle. Calcium splinters on impact, do you,
running through pits of hysterical sun, posing for
photographers, a ring of cops around the neck.
If you feel weighed down don't worry, it's only
the price-tag in your mouth, stored in police files
as wealth jangles in pockets and you study
what words mean when you don't understand,
when you don't know you can't be sure. Meanwhile,
you wake up in the morning and pebbles have not

grown in your throat, suggesting the five differences
between granite and cows. This isn't hysteria.
Its as rational as anyone's likely to get, as pebbles
split, scratch toads. It isn't a question, not even
of wealth. Just when and is he ever, does he ever
intend to get those leather hands off my throat.

There's got to be something to do about the hole in the door, the paint on the walls *cowslip. jagwort. helix. monksbeard) the replacement of stains* to unhook the telephone calls. send them free, skidding. watch them scraping the skybrood. then fill in the holes. **whatever. grimly count your pennies.**

(and whatever satisfaction that might **such a pity. and toads there, waiting in shadows.** the view from the window bears little relation to <u>*bitten and sulph'd*</u> have you ever been to the end of the street. take a good hard look at the imitations. they're growing.

Just going down there to post a letter
Left at the siren
Down there down that / gone down
From letter to letter
Vessel to vessel
Latched
Locked
The vessel
Loaded
Remain in the vessel (dyou think it will
Rain
Its mad here mad to
Severe love
Cling to that
Will break still love
Steal away
Loaded
Locked
Down there down that/ its all a
Gate
M   st
E
Locked / shut
My love
Away
Throbbing in
                    Drift<u>wood</u>

        <u>A few ghosts</u>
From vessel to vessel
On impact
Rainballs burst (in
                    nettles and bronze
                    intact

[10]

Certain young aristocrats are photographed pushing trolleys on sink estates as evidence of their compassion. Its great fun dropping TVs on their heads. The shape || that || it was it ass || never at is called dog-s. Monksbeard. A stain. And then out to buy records.

The houses are startling geometry (*telephone:* yes? <u>rainpit.</u> <u>redmarsh. lipfuck.</u> no. couldn't think what (like snapgrin *the houses so bountiful. everybody there. at sewing.* an axe embedded in the head reveals such splendours. though the neighbours look on aghast.

(CALLING ALL DOGS . . . .

Its to do with watching TV and making all kinds of phonecalls.
To leave the house not unreasonable[   ]but
**unthinkable. whoever it is keeps writing in chalk on the
pavements. and buckets of stars** the house unravelable

*Into the bindering household   so that I could my sleep /
the noise comes this way (hear myself in my own voice
rats   made well as he*

                              THE STREET IS A BONE.

The Rose (2000)

pop stars on Holloway Road

a lifetime. the body named
as bubbles are
in a pan at boiling point
& overflow
is cinnabar. its like
standing outside the Odeon
wondering whether
to cross the road, buy a paper
to shelter from the rain —
all adverts cancelled
& thieves retreat
into shelters, not apples
& cigarettes to minimise appeal
intensity. like diet pepsi
hurts y teeth
then its gone, like the address,
the figure in the window,
like pop's been shite for years
anyway. think of it. who
are Blur
kidding.

so cough up the painting
& gold, settles in the lungs
reproduces
life that feeds on sulphur.
so live
where even animals would die.
so live behind broken clouds
& maps, worn, hazy
at the edges, burnt even
the places to live
breathing.

the window won't open. the
cold night fog brings ocean
invisible creatures
to crack open lips
& heart, to flood
in & out. beauty. fuck
it. lipgrind,
tonguemusk. more clouds?
just buy some ketamine,
swim down 3rd Avenue,
the shore-line, clamber
up into London,
aquatic mammals. serenade
the tube and grin unhumour,
cold and green.

Painting, painting, pouring
on the oil, hands stained
cigarettes, lips, methadone,
stained with Kings Cross
puked the next day away
Radio 4, hands shaking.

My hatred of the rich
is non-judgemental,
non-random, an obelisk
to drag across a map
of all the places you visited
the sparks that showered stars.
wankers turn blue
in bricked up rooms
and trains pass. property
speculation, value calculated

on the length of vibration
the chaldean discus
trembling in fingers
throw pebbles at
flickering windows,
move in the light of the traffic.

All these speculators
nicking what they
think's dead cool.
naked, or in jacket,
financial expletives,
rents predict astronomy: on
the street again, lets see,
one jacket, three boots
& that's the lot. boho
themeparks the world over,
shovel the homeless
out of Tompkin's Square
& no-one's surprised.
just what exactly is
a buffalo girl,
where does she hide.

so collect the spirits
of dead capitalists
haunting the tube, abstract
gnosis. better
go shoot, anything,
work on a painting
for three years till
the image coats your gut,
a jacket, all

kinds of warm weather. step
into postcards, be
stupid or glam.
retire to a factory,
write shit. mail it out,
wait in the blue light
of your flickering cell
pulsates with 30,000
years
of sexual prediction
& beyond that
some kind of
stone you're carrying
scraping a path
through London mud
& traffic, gridlock.

or the train stops in tunnel
for the benefit of tourists
who accumulate in vast numbers
on the corner of Whitehall
just for the purpose
of scaring the pigeons
& conversing with bricks
literally, mirrors
that shimmer
with the eye peering
out, unknown
to beast and humanity
& the river that echoes
beneath your boots flagstones
carries sulphur,

bedrock of strange life,
plants, solar ice.

           ∼

freely associate
with the variables the numbers
exist all round town
like bridges like river
of their own invention
freely to go in one door
out another out a different building
in the lights that hang in windows
in faces

           ∼

them plaster faces
put them in yr mouth they
                w a r m
        something sound like pebbles
        underwater   almost
        pebbles   almost

             h e a t   s i g h s
             (patron of thieves and seas

           ∼

or then again
there's always the possibility

of Charing Cross
the fall to the knees the singing
as bubbles
in a pan at boiling

slogans (cuz when maths is broken
            we eat it

        ∽

ah the plate full of numbers
laced with memory and sauce
bubbling warmly under
                    bracken rocks:

the silver headed brook
the invasion of Oxford St
the naming of plants and animals
the naming of streets and planets
the invocation of corpuscles
the feeding of cells

        ∽

freely associate
in the sounds that faces make
in nets and geography

            ministers and molecules

(light reflected off several windows

        ∽

its best to walk in the shop
(spell of invisibility)

dress down, but don't stink

shove the goods
whatever you want
down y pants, under y hat
into y bone,
                walk out, recall
you've done nothing wrong

get to the tube, or bone, whatever
damn fast
ha. now you can eat.

          ∾

do you kiss on a first date

          ∾

broke the stone open and
communication

(we ate those golden things
(do you kiss on a first date
(bah—I'll pull y teeth out
(so cough me
(in my hands here have
(down y pants, under y hat
(into y bones

          ∾

meet me on Oxford St
we'll go into Borders

steal everything.

For Bob,
Cobbing Through the Soundhole,
Where Cobbing IS

IS A VERB IS ::: the pupil of the eye is ::: to gate to verse ::: to
reach over, sunrise, to seize, to live through ::: casting metal,
pouring oil ::: to METAL to scry to ::: flow to wilder to ::: to lament
wailer ::: to invoke spider ::: to under ::: to stand under to ::: take
wing ::: to turn the ground ::: well ::: spring ::: to brighten ::: the
palmprint, casting, seizing over ::: VOWELPIT ::: to turn the :::
turn the ::: old ::: duplicator ::: handle to ::: turn ::: one's role ::: to
roll ::: to reach over, sunrise ::: to roll the ground ::: one's life the
::: mark on the paper the ::: sound ::: emitted ::: the skyline ::: to
sing ::: is a verb ::: to signal ::: the vowelpit ::: from vessel to vessel
::: to signal ::: palmprint ::: to signal ::: to mouth START
MOTHFLOOM ::: is a verb is ::: MOTHFLOOM (arising in the rift
between mind and tongue, thought and word) black noise :::
resides in other elements ::: more like itself ::: making the poem
::: more like itself ::: in mind and tongue ::: in thought and word
::: in vowelpit ::: casting metal, pouring oil ::: to brighten, to seize,
to love through ::: the soundhole ::: in vowelpit ::: in black noise :::
in flicker noise light ::: cocophonise ::: to love through ::: all the
words in any language spell ::: what burst what blue flame ::: that
rinky dink that bebopalula ::: what no century is ::: them precious
stones them hole in the ground them ::: pictures ::: liberation :::
MY LIFE IN A HOLE IN A soundflow ::: wavecrash red::: throat
o SEA wavesound ::: wordblow ::: its all sperm its ::: word toss and
scatter ::: noise ingested ::: throttlestar ::: in your throat to speak
of ::: to enter them words to walk around the ::: burst in bees of :::
swallow down ::: from vessel, ova, water ::: to brighten, the
palmprint, casting, seizing over ::: to turn the skyline ::: as the
sound of ::: to flicker noise ::: in comet hair ::: in stamp stamp n
kickfoot ::: in the pupil of the eye ::: to reach over, sunrise, to
seize, to live through ::: MY LIFE IN A liberation wavecrash :::
resides ::: poetry ::: now ::: more like itself ::: in other elements :::
reside ::: elements (thorngust) ::: elements (mothfloom) ::: in the

turn ::: in the hands ::: in elements ::: resides ::: poetry ::: in
skyline ::: emerges ::: to signal ::: from vowelpit ::: to mouth ::: in
element resides other ::: more like itself ::: resides ::: in marks on
paper ::: emitted ::: skyline ::: elements turning ::: the ground
handle ::: the role ::: resides ::: in wingtake ::: in wellspring ::: to
turn the ground ::: bone ::: muscle ::: nerve ::: blood ::: brain :::
poetry resides

Notes on Heresy (2000–2001)

Tom O'Bedlam

Rag it
Hungry
Rend it
Naked

Book of senses

Self forsaken
Thought is sky
Will ever walk it
Night-stripped
Love-lipped
Thought is sky
Is senses wing
Is oxlet
Ragwort
Waken
Senses five &
Rend it naked
Burning
Love-lipped
Journey

Rag and wretch
The humdrum
Watered
Lark-rock open
Senses five
& forty days with
Beggar's staff
By sea or land
   Is cold to drink
The fury-glass
The standing pool
   Is city-meat
From newt to tadpole
   Spawn to man
Is charged with fire
Is lark-rock breathing
Myrtle-stone
To mark the city
Cross the palm
With silver glass
& scarlet ring
Of poisoned sense
Of sea or land
Will ever walk it
Devil-lipped

Love-bodied

Swallow
Standing pool
Is cold

Swallow
Standing pool is
Cold is
Broken in
The journey-night
The stinking soul
Is obsolete (from)
Cash-toothed ghosts
A-kicking Tom (s)
A cold

Want cash want cash
& murder Tom(s)
A cold

Want cash want cash
And murder
Tom's a
Cold
Lip-silver
Hold his poison (ed)
Sea or land
To mark the faces
Tom has slept
To keep his wide-eye
                Fancy

Ten days I haven't
Eaten
Ten days
I
Don't
Talk shit
Or mark the
Carving
Money-meat
His book of senses
Open

Tom's a cold
A lamb
A lamper veil
And break the shine
Cos Tom's a cold
A stinking skein
A lambsbread moth
To break the curses
Stone the crawling
Common-sense of
Lambstone
Lambthrone
Breaking
Curses belching
Threats of law
A London stone
Around the neck of
Tom's a stinking
Skin of shine
A broken
High-tide
Juika
Curses
Curses on the
        Whip the
Lambthrone
Break it
Bleat through
Foxglove
Hartbeat
Flicker
Out
The cursing breath

Of common sense
A lamb's throw
Breaking
Throats
Of curses
(flowers

Defects in the Structure of the State

That the leaves fall late
& float, old drunks, up
turned
& vanish
& the air is a flame
of rubble, construction

1330: tell me what do you wish
I
do not wish   what
are you   I am not
the broken country
the drone of ages   in rubble   are you
oil of lunacy   I am not (1340) on a slow fire
                           that the leaves are
gimme 15p &   turned   & vanish
burn the hedges   cross water
like strange sparrows do   red-robed   as lorries pass
don't   on a slow fire   in deep time

                           establish songs   commercial centres
                           I am not
                           am nameless
                           nameless rubble (have refused
                                     the plea of lunacy

                           but tell but me
                           from where do you come

                           from trade-routes, from nowhere
                           a spark or a light
                           like strange sparrows

The letter A (for us this is not a crime
       or C (is musk, ambergris, bruised lingum
       or F (

           gimme 15p &
           tell me the business

but what but tell me
the falling leaves the
blood of a pigeon the
brain of a fox but
what do you wish   I
                  do   the broken country
drone   un-red
old drunk

for alef-beta
for schwerster katrei

(1989: the resident don't want their poisonous water

that we turn   & vanish
red-robed   cross water
to transcend institutional frameworks

but what that
the leaves are
vanish   & old drunks
float, up turned

like strange euphorbium, lodestone & sulphur

1330
1270
1550
1545
1307
1340
1544 (autonomous groups of involuntary poor

                              cross water dryshod
                              walk a yard above ground

Not from round here are you
(if you give me a piece of money I'll

caaaarve

(the glass
till windows
where you keep your face
& break

& scratch in
deed
as if fingernails
litter
dreams   my "me"
is they

won't charge the earth

secret words, secret hoardings
illegal persons
pass through calendars
into leaves,
                dates,
                        wheels
imagine
what are you
I am not
(the park is on fire

[34]

if 1495 is easy
if 201 is the same
year, the names on the litter
change, is all, te naming
the seasons
brick up
a fear of loving
translated to history
where names are etched out
are sewn in the voice
the fabric, the logic
is wrong

      & chase the net of ghouls
      all money is

will brick up the gates
the dangerous rhythms
the ashes, the river
will fill all mouths
that talk wild talk
      & rain he said yes
      there is a
      spot of ink my
      face could
      scrub the
      shells to keep
      the voice in locked &

            earth
            warm
            flood
            locked
            shell

poor
devils that we are

Lyric Poetry: Surveillance

"Poetry is always somewhere. Everywhere repressed, this poetry springs up everywhere. Brutally put down, t is reborn in violence. It plays muse to rioters, informs revolt and animates all great revolutionary carnivals for a while, until the bureaucrats consign it to the prison of hagiography"—Raoul Vaneigem.

The city boundaries have their origins in motions of trade. The herm stone, the boundary stone between two cities, sacred to Hermes, patron of thieves and poets, would be the site at which trade exchanges would take place. At a certain point the site of trade moved into the centre of the city, creating the market and in effect turning the whole place inside out. The old boundary was now hemmed in by the walls of the city, and everything that took place was defined by the act and speech of trade.

In Charles I's reign there were whipping posts for beggars every few hundred yards in London.

"Thou hast many bags of money, and behold now I come as a thief in the nght, with my sword drawn in my hand, and like a thief as I am I say 'deliver your purse! Deliver, Sirrah! Deliver or I'll cut your throat"—Abiezer Coppe.

To use no violence on any citizen
Or animal on the surface of the ground

at the border (**imagined**

          "moder
                  nlaw   **ss**

at this side   *stun border*
mountains &   *goods, & hands*
then cannons   *offered*
<u>over there</u>   *guitars*
<u>even heather</u>   *grass*
wired
as one year
<u>becomes</u>
a closing eye
becomes   **daisyknot**
<u>words in</u>   & fist-traders
mouth becomes   travel music-line
our customs (games   uphold myth
our gibberish   twist in possession
give offence   *of full passport*
in eye
closed
a <u>different</u> law   **COPPER MOUTH**
prevents   <u>**& silence**</u>   (necklace
speech   of wind
in approaching   on rock
     ledges
shadows
this silence
cavernous   a second
hiss   becomes a decade
                         a closing eye
                         where wind collects
                         in <u>*faustspools*</u>

all recorded
hands in pocket
waved through

"enjoy your stay" **(spurt)**

violent
river
smoke

the territory

alien   canning town
glass   mile hand
river   hole burn
                             1460

all recorded. all strange

                    [sir. I am a stranger in this town. I am
                    eaten well at the flings. come let me
                    be your money. be your land. your
                    paper.   come write with
        me
                    come bone my jaw

flint residue under human streets & silence
re-ordered

the territory   stone   glass   smoke
wired   passengers   programme
clouds
glyphs

"let me be your money"

voices
echo
st ones

at the
mirthowl
eve
wir as
bee becon
cus
owl
our givmir   *flint residue*
cus   under
iceclaws   voices
give   under
evehiss   voicejaw
claws   *come live*
gi mir   *and I will be your land*
thowl   will
                    bound hole
                    burn
                    oil of lunacy
                    like strange sparrows
                    twist in possession
                                    (a choice
                    divide
                    to excite, impulse
                                    (motion flowing
                    flow: liquid, a teaching, an amber
                    to divide, to break
                    the drone of ages
                    to consume I
                    to be that wall
                    I could be that wall
                    it's a bad thing for a girl
                    for a boy to be a wall

heartstir

hearthair

[earth]

like 3 a.m.
the dogtaxi sblaring
y
living
wanton
kissing
like rain is
footsteps
beakprint

neon

[obsolete semantics of nightown
some kind of illegal
drinking club is intended   my wanton ribbon
angle of vision   kiss my
is taxi blaring
skewed   hurtle

                                  miss my
                                  [riot is closure

                                  [earth
                                  teethkisses
                                  my flesh my
                                  my neon my
                                  plaguey neon
                                          p-lagueing 3 a.m.

[42]

hearthair [will rent a simple room

earth   air   kisses

[obscure semantics
of nightown
of mantic
air in   & announce the cracks
ribboned kisses   the cracks in the earth
earth my   are the voice
flesh in   *flint residue*
heart in   *under*
heart is   *voices*
static   *under*
                          voicejaw
                          come live
                          and I will be your land
                          will
                          bound hole
semantic   *burn*   by kisses, the voice is

below: coughs, gulps, bubbles, growls   [a network of streets
                                              is the palm
such architecture
rolling cars and nettles, telephone interrupts
                                      is stars

                                [

[43]

stars and slurry: <u>taxi</u>
           disappears
           the corner is rain
           wheel is Fentiman
           Road the light is
               on it will <u>rain</u>
                  <u>god</u>

horsilver: rust in   whipn tomcrack
tomcrack   broken
broken   cold as   hearthair teeth
ravens strangely
turning   turn the   toms a cold
broken   distant
horsehead silver   silver
rust and rise as   rusted

<u>money</u>
<u>mystery</u>   rusted tom a
<u>money</u>   bedlam blistered
<u>mystery</u>   rust the rain
                    a circles tom
                    the taxi
                    ravens
                    [**burning**]

Confessional Poetry

In 1649, the year the king was executed, Abiezer Coppe stood up at the pulpit of a church somewhere in central London, and swore without interruption for an hour. Clearly a lost avant-garde classic. George Fox, however, was horrified that "men and women . . . should be brought to place their religion in revelling, roaring, drinking, whoring . . . and the fearfulest cursing that hath been heard".

And a few years later, Ann Baites of Morpeth was accused of having transformed herself into cat, hare, greyhound and bee

> *I shall go into a hare*
> *With sorrow and sighing and mickle care*
> *And I shall go in the Devil's name*
> *Aye, till I come home again*

The hare: one of only two edible animals ever tabooed in Britain. The hare in the saying. The shadow in the meaning.

of Morpeth 1673 held to her mouth
a hare said my imps names are dream
in say no to eating of that flesh
my imps names are vinegar tom

(said confess

after several minutes was taken and put in a bag in the earth in a fire.
was put in a needle was broken was put in a hood. was thorn hand
bastard Ishmael. was judged by the tooth of the vicious was stretched on
the law of the mighty was picked clean by roosters and blues. was
ground to dust was melted to glass held fast in the walls of the mighty.
was a mirror was held broken and fast was the glass and what was
drunken

ann bait 1673 confess morpeth the dreaming
longblack coat that devil protect them call
it god or crack to call the bone a hare
to say no to eating of that flesh to say
it hurts to be [   ] but announce ann
bait will form a cat then bee a hare to
run them will not see there she in hair held
up to [   ] smile

been walking
from Hare's
Walk to
Berwick St been
given a piece
of money a
circle of bread
been given two
bottles of ink-
drink of ink to
make my vein
a glass of
poem been
made and
hurts it walking
leave a print
and scared at
night for what
my path
may cross

[47]

she moves through the fair
honestly it's a sight to
weave consensus
of window broken
where a face should be

what to say to break that power and tawdry magic
is old newspapers on Berwick St (are)
depositories of sound arrange such
awareness is geometry

        ghosts / characters / fictions
          burst their paper
           flame to inhale
            hoof-ash
              & grow tumours
                what fracture in the teeth
                  any city you like
                    has shops are dust or
                      dream-hole

she moves through the fair
and has been doing for years
and longing develops habits
and join the dots yourself
every solid is in theory
reality is

every day I invent a name to live inside

who the hell is vinegar tom talking in tongues and dropping me in it

the hour of dawn is trespass
err where you live
in a knuckle of the river
talks at night

my imp's name will walk through the fair with

when I was a jackal machine I split minds

when I was a wave
a tower on a hill
a hole in the ground
I would cackle and roar at your jewellery and riches
                              (you bourgeois sons of bitches

with my bitchbreath I whelping
nail my talk to
ocean leaves

                              windows
                              every day I scry

[49]

every day I say where the hell is imp number
one way of being fantastic every day I sniff my
nails (skymoss) everysay who the hell are you
poet number three with eyes stitched and
everyday I walk through the door and punch my
way through what ties together lips and tongue till
sex is theory and time a liquid to wash my what
time is its 3 a.m. and we've all drowned
everyday I get out of town my bracken-imp will
stalk his voice with flames and ropes everyday I
say stop burning me as she upleapt she
clawed righting ann bait of morpeth

1673 held to her mouth a meaning everyday she
move through the thorn-fair everysay she speak
like crow-meaning thend o v me a n i ng iss no I
is e me no I is imp number one is a crackle in
the earth is hearing hare and thornflood everyday
endeth and walk through ann bait in the evening
moves over the lake dryshod a yard above
meaning everyday I say confess and claw writing
a cackle in the eye everysay meaning iss I is
mm is meaning is thorn-nnoise and is everyday
the meaning is noise as she move through the
fair dryshod a mile above ground took it and sold

Poisons, their Antidotes (2001–2003)

The Management Consultant Has Gone for Lunch

walked fr Vauxhall cross
to obelisk the
GULL
to Cleopatra the GULL
on sunshine on
pastry round
the GUT-MOUTH
walk
the GULL-WALK
up villiers
to cross and
ON

up west the
rampires and hellrakes
and leaves   falling
and light   falling
and   falling
and
        walking on
        un-shine

cough twice and
ON

on cough-blister
walking on
cheek-blister

but then

sunlight
parc mercuric
sparrows

          orange berries
          emergenc

the parc was
something to
to spout
GULLS

to bind the eyes
intact in

tin sparrows

          the dead-line

walking on
the masonry quarter
in all these rooms these
pits of glass
its hard to see the

FUCK LIKE A CANNIBAL
in veins you could swim down
in don't be so rude
in what the
          outside
the world
          is
walking on
          gloat-face
is walking on un-shine

up the charing cross
& derail at
Greek St. derailed
by restaurant hours
&
who the hell are these
lunching on
daymob
of

& onward. gullblack
is Bakunin's secret network of
ROAST PIGS
the betrayals are

arches &
bridges built of

glass-sharp
squirrel-fox
shards
      from clay build a monster
      to walk with. only at noon

night-cries
abandon the word
for a dose of celebrity theory
up west

the wyrd

up to Greek St

derailed

    nightcries

I like drinking coffee
and talking about swearing

MOONSPIT
hieroglyphic
the betrayals are
head or heels
[Bakunin, toothless & haunted
& equate the war
with some child repeatedly
gobbing in his own face
for a whole half hour
mercuric

nets

that stars are
bankrupt
& magazines
will keep us warm

IGNITION

as we develop a fear of
GULLS
of what they know what we don't know

& this is

so shut it

o once I had a money
blew it all out
on tobacco &

silver lining
[splashveins

       anarchism
       was just a suggestion
       redsky at night
       means we're in

choke-pears
shopkeeps

abandon the world
for a host of breaking suns
for a

splashvein

[up tottenham court was all
field &

where I live
all marshgas:

no-one will consider

the import

the nation is

chokepears, rampires & hellrakes

where I live

all copbreath

    is
    is
everybody is

      orange berries

with a dose of
patriotic
    blister

and leaves   crawling
and light   crawling
and

everybody is
just like everybody is
just like

VOICE ONE: blah
VOICE TWO: blah

walked fr vauxhall cross
only the footsteps the
crackling sky
lit up &
torn

as paper is
this paper

rainstuffed on Greek St
recalls
        terror
or was that litter

[weary & tired, in shop-doorways
tattered daub the sky
with one more coffee. Old Compton St
teach me new swearwords
tearing the tears from

VOICE ONE: blank

mercury is

on new oxford st
Bakunin in feather
& windows

for a dose of

mercury is
        fireground
for a dose of

what I say is

up Berwick St
for secondhand CDs
& sanctity is

MOONSPIT

[or was that backgammon

VOICE ONE: hold out till the engines come

IMAGE: hand, outstretched
        a lack, the face of

VOICE FIVE: laughter laughter

VOICE ONE: lennon mccartney

VOICE TWO: "The bomb is the echo of your cannon, trained
upon our starving brothers; the shriek of those maimed and torn
in your corporate slaughterhouses; tis the shadow of the crisis,
the rumbling of suppressed earthquake"
IMAGE: blank

IMAGE: laughter

IMAGE: blank

up west
for a dose of

sunlight
parc mercuric
sparrows
        orange berries
        emergenc

the parc was
something to
to spout
GULLS

to bind the eyes
intact in
tin sparrows

        the dead-line

walking on
the masonry quarter
in all these rooms these
pits of glass
its hard to see the

FUCK LIKE A CANNIBAL
in veins you could swim down
in don't be so rude
in what the
        outside
the world
        is

walking on
       gloat-face
is walking on un-shine

IMAGE: blank

IMAGE: blank

IMAGE: tin sparrows
IMAGE: blank

IMAGE: gulls

IMAGE: blank

IMAGE: blank

IMAGE: blank

it is not terror
the sadness is

the

Paul Verlaine reads poems on Old Compton St

(said) starspin, yr mouth is spitstars
(said)
     ack, searise, cityraise (said)
illplay,
     ore (said) dance machine
   con-ill (said) pee lute
kell itch
     key pain
          ka
(said) oil brute, eat soil
(said) oil chant, delete / play
               on Dean St corner, al true
               where media stops where
    breathing begins
              stop: calcify: form
                      nul
                    treason
    if you draw a line from_____ to _____
    your ribs will align wth
    cracks will form will
    Berwick will Beak will Frith will
    myth crack, mouth rack / will
              & monuments are
Verlaine read poems &
the commune was betrayed
buried, up to its neck
in pavements, walked on, kicked in
& what year is this   *sense ray*
what street is this (the table grain   *ore key*
        a refuge, in candle-light
      in reason
         in spitstars

fading, the voices fade
kell itch, key pain. this
is information. what we want is class war.

this report to be slipped inside paperback books in Waterstones
my life has aways been
on the corner of two worlds
I saw what I still see   oi brute
I am not the only one of my kind   nul treason
                                           oi brute
                                        nul treason

Expulsions (on Marchmont St with coffee)

"I am not George Bush"
      overheard this   and coffee
"I do not have
           to wake up in the morning
I do not decide"
      was saying this
to stop it
      removing my coffee
did not   awaken me   my ink
      was what my face was not
to eat   or close the door
    or say
      I love
or what   (to say   o
Bakunin   Heraclitus
and all the rest in

      coughing
    hair up
is there more coffee
   or are we still talking
     the coffee cup   & steam
   where cloth is   piss
    hidden   or hands
   with what a face is not   or
  what
     does it mean   to
say   "I am not George Bush
    I do not have to think"
      for what does
broken in to Marchmont St
the steam   where coffee is
     where lips are
   this

is hidden   I am not am I
coffee or is it
        a vocal (wants me to leave
                    did not
awaken or   breaking
decision
                to drink some coffee
to say   Bakunin
to say   Heraclitus
                    to drink some ink
                    behind the hand is
where the
            piss
is where the
lips are

no I am not
and as for you
        this is a
coffee shop
        fundamentally
                for eating for
closing the door
        and steam is
                for listing
                things to love
like coughing   hair
and
        not talking
what   a hand does
not mean   this is
        what the
not piss

                    even coffee

                                    does not

                if you are not
George Bush
                it does not mean
I think and
piss
        the things you
imagine
            the death of really evil men

yeh I hope you die
George Bush
(can't say plainer than
        evil
streets
        are trembling lips
are love
        where milk is steam and
lips are words to love   (o
Heraclitus
                    would not
this coffee
I
        don't want to
leave
        and what will
steam the
                    door
will say
        am not
awaken this
                    is not a face

is
        Marchmont St
a place to
                tremble or
love
        decide to
stay

Poisons, their Antidotes

1.

at Turnmill St, in
<u>deed</u>

    (fernie brae)
of grass-green silk
(ilka tate
    fifty siller bells

<u>fear of strangers "that name does not belong to</u>
(locked:)hail

in brass howls (ona)
red wind:
churning over(   ) bodies / wind

2.

imagine a clockmaker
split-

imagine all the persons
eating raw starz raw
popup
        waistrel

the end of the land is

light my, gobshite

        I wish I had a word for
        tideclamps/ slashpalms/ furnace
        (the end of the world is
        boring boring
        tide-laps-

        ticktick-

        tideclamps-

(m-way silence-

(rainslick punctured 25 sparrows-

(now-

3.

surveillance shard-

act out tongue below camera
tongueact: this is/ webshine

now pitch a stutter/ carve it
cars insist on
streetgob: caughtin
lights   : the street is owls is
                                 (mazeclamped)
                                 split hydrogen daisies
                                 is
footsteps: the sucking spider in Westminster

4.

locked: (boil

6.

sparrows in jected
it is making maps/ in
locked: boil
in taxilight in

soundblock:
for three days now
a
                (spine
. . . . /everything
blisters:
split n all of feathers
bursts: oh to turn around
        win big money
          spend it like

strike blister ((
for three days now
scratching
              in

& that's just a word for
sparrows-

7.

        police lines (meaning

        entryway to
        popstarz (light my
        one more fuck pig
        this is an (

(   )
shard-
rooms where diagrams rust-

tidelap-

police line (meaning-

        shoot out
        seek &
        (celebrities cancelled
        (puerile/ sneak a
        SMILE, YOU'RE ON
5 minutes 28 seconds to boil a pot of water
break window (winter)

boil, seconds
8th December

8.

-rainslick punctured 25 sparrows

-m-way silence

-wet pavements, loose bricks, things

particles expanding
light desperation
end at
        streetsounds of
Baghdad
emerge (cynical
        bone   tourista   load
(we should be)
blast
        with
(   )
1=1 is
what we want is
Donald Rumsfeld Tommy Franks
their blood
the end of the world is
(listening to)
after the riot watched us on TV
on
        "its plain our civilization has an obsession with shortening time" on
thorny wire   *the city in these*
                                   the police are real
                                   your favourite band will now be

buy it now be
boilfink: everyone in

(change): got ten p got more than
sing:
sing:

I love the sound of
this years idiot smile s
a box of things to
eat and fuck

                       overpriced (use your debit card to
glue rib to
American
idiot
box of

o'erpriced

things to
glue
persons
(wet bricks . . . . . . <u>loose/</u> behind the eyes

5 minutes 28 seconds to
think about
cashback/

sliced clocks are-
could never happen here-
our-
freedom of speech is-
burn baby burn-
my lips are-
stained-

with speech is-
all our tongues are-
wish-
but had a word for-
lips-
but all our tongues are-
wish-
but had word-
for slice-
for-
clock our freedom is-
a murderer's fucking head-

9.

how many lives
has the government
burned
contamination of
reason or
names are frayed
around the ingratiating table
demands your hooked hands
by reason of
what
red sky at night means
the earths on fire
gold prices rise as
lies in parliament today
resume echo itch
those who require life
would live without
new moon contamination
those who would are
corridors
open to existence doubt
his howled hand
hook burns
the living room
lethal virus
the new middle caste is
BP announces
megawatt officials
eat the north
developments in business
discuss to protect
thwack impact

revealed
cormorants croak in
tourist potential
at a dry rot level
o new moon
one of the darkest
claim a free strong wind
a barren nation
to read and rot
is virtue
is gorged loop
is sharpening wires
o new fanged head

10. MARCHING MUSIC

HAVE TONGUE WILL TRAVEL —
& WHAT HAVE YOU DONE YOU —
VIOLENCE IS SENTIMENT —
A FUCK-COLOURED PLUME —
& WHAT HAVE YOU DONE YOU —
FAIRIES BOILED —
HAVE TONGUE WILL TRAVEL —
AS GARETH GATES SAYS —
ONE TWO 3 FOUR —
VOWELS INTERRUPTED —
STAINS ON THE CHANCELOR —
SETAG SETAG —
& WHAT HAVE YOU DONE YOU —
GATES AND WALLS —
SUCH IS THE COWARDICE —
FAIRIES BOILED —
RED SKY YELLOW SKY —
OI BLUSH THORN PRANCE —
& WHAT HAVE YOU DONE YOU —
ONE 2 THREE FOUR —
STAINS ON THE CHANCELOR —
BIRD NOISE WORM NOISE —
RED SKY YELLOW SKY —
HAVE TONGUE WILL TRAVEL —
& WHAT HAVE YOU DONE YOU —
SHIT-FACED GOON —
SUCH IS THE CWARDICE —
RED SKY YELLOW SKY —
AS GARETH GATES SAYS —
VIOLENCE IS SENTIMENT —
ONE TWO THREE 4 —
CLAW TRACKS BONE —

LITTLE BIRDS NOTHING —
SULPHUR IS SENTIMENT —

11.

(this speech made by Mr Blair, Glasgow, Feb 15th 2003 . . . .

I am Tony Bl : a right moral p / inst war : ording ience
ye!

and some : equences are a : protest? : I ask t : opularit, rice
of : re/ 500

are one : arted so : are con ever : be / I exist : ision an : is the
: is not : it is a : number / the numb (I tell y —): e victim :
een but — telligen : is moth? (ugh it) ortant t : for go

I am Tony I live in honour b : he cost less t : still le : f peace :
n blood re on ou : want us : o see the : if we c : t is in : n
power a countr r democ this I ut comet of convi : han the ss
than : is : then : but thes : r tv scr : to be in (I tell y) victim
tongue of moral ass dest eek to a : the ter

not only : onflict : f people hate st : rting so thin : any y
rules of the c vice how ruction void war : rorists : us invad :
ople bac : d April able hat ot the ons of : do so wi : of war :
must li (in pitch and soot in turds and piss in viper bile in
squirming spawn . . .

I am anemical : ath moneygents wi't tongue lict f vice ho :
pril : pitch a ming spa

ye!

t rice o : t ision : ye vict go I am y rules f war mu er bile

I am Ton : and som im een b tony bla peace n n power o
testin mora ir I liv blood re more im just a l ass de void the
ons in turds

inst war I ask n ever b : the numb : oth ugh our : be he ant
us o : the learch : in pitch a the ons of m dof war must li ine
hat so wi : o ming spain turds : and piser bile : in squirnd
soot in vip ording : opulari I exis : I tell moral p : protest : o
arc co : number : ugh!

Filth Screed (2003–2004)

All poetry that does not testify to an awareness of the radical falsity of the established forms (of life) is faulty. Understand prosody via black bloc tactics.* No-one has yet spoken a language which is not the language of those who establish, enforce, and benefit from the facts. Language is conservative. Its conservatism issues (a) from its utilitarian purpose, (b) from the fact that the memory of a person, like that of humankind, is short.

* archaic reference, unexplained.

stood—
once for 25 minutes watched an owl peel a mouse—
in london we have a street—
fleas have bitten its self like the time I went blind on Wardour St—
when the trees all flickered like men —
stood once for 25 minutes waiting for a chance to move in the nest—
as if biting —
a lamp & vice versa —
as if biting —
stood once and watched a mouse, the fur and skin—
mess of maps (peeled, clasped in beak,   in—
London's trees, the voices leak—
drip drip drip, like bat soup—
or ant   eros—

a n t s o r e s —
but if they hadn't droppt bombs he'd still have his arms and legs —
the key word this morning is owl peel —
those fuzzy things are people —
today I will chew, till juice runs —
the key word this morning is fuzzy thing —
screech screech screech then shut your face —
his arms & legs —
the moving trees flicker —
the key word is rational, derangement —

he feels like a stranger here   sorry for the country   big dog —

           sketch
      a definition of
              infinity is a
      suck bracket
           pinned
      history slurp your
                button
           horn

      ∿

owl machines :

thats vice, burning
on Lambeth Road   /musk twirl
                              /in human bridges
                         /& accountants

deadly machines—

questionable savagery. this sullen
skull job, bright land

same old thing—
tongue stuck in eye—
kiss—
on the arse a tiny—
flags—
lines of them—
flags—
taste like shit like—
lines of them—
glimpse—
thats social life in London. as tongue enters. a colony or a spasm.
    kiss him. stick your cock in his ear

thin suns bleat
a black dot inside
the world has stabilized
moved on, solidified
an iris gap seizure
totale split))

mouse sounds / river cluster

his opened mouth
pours particle assortment
rotating in his hand
"they gathered on Kennington Park
fell into a great noise :
the city a lattice of nameless fibre
seen from a distance
a flutter   a willow
a siren moan

a lattice of swallow-screech, a
waiting room, some christians
    some lions, some
        obvious points

a king
of bitten clay
a scarab scrape
a scrape of water
a imp split

a king is a used rat
no, not even a rat, more a burnt finger
a scratch dog
a bone twitch
a skull in the supermarket
almost like in a bucket at the seaside

this is a shop spurt yellow gas
we drink it sliced
in a furnace
the question is who made them killers
clipping hugging imbracing
in a strange manner
o sunflower
under all this heap of ashes
like a drunken man
chewing down the loop slice
o weary of, stuff
nice demure barren
now staining honourable persons
& fence fiends

fly track
negative to negative
magnetic repulse
a glyph jerk
shrink into suck time
on all paws
raise entry
groan display
one fly will split
a tiny eruption
into open mouths
shudder star
amoebic surveillance
hanging
fault
another mouth stapled
magnet rip
all the cops in this room
are blue
scratched on the wall
with a knife
as data
threaded
insect cog
decode the symbols
as piss in his face

at 9.38 you hear voices
they say what is this

laugh now
this is a shop
tie a ribbon round your
glass scraps
you like these sirens
you like these
glass scraps
this is a
blue bottle
this is a
skin clock
you like these
long green pills
sulphur
kiss skin clock
they have set up
glass scraps
you like these
spit boy
sirens
sulphur glass scraps
clock time
kiss sulphur clock time
kiss scrap sulphur pills
you like this
they say what is this
spools
what do you love
siren clench kiss clock
who do you love

in the slashed cry
sulphur
on his fingers
this is a shop
who do you

they have not yet driven him down
he has no machine inside his mouth
his name is not Lord Falconer

alembic strip neutral. wiring
        in the prison brain : snout
     expands, a jewellery rip exploded
downtown Dagenham, combustion snort.

he collapsed in frame distort job split.
   do him, skull job split stagger
extinguish   Piccadilly   smack beam

the bus stops here. and walking
even that is unpermitted—

enabled history on the ant crawl
                    a cut voice
          swarm   a red disk
          split the minimum you can spend
     on conversation   or sting removal
       a faint orange stench
in from the coast
               try a night attack;   call me peroxide
        or just drill for numbers
     eye rift gull dust
            synapse lamp   stutter gap
open throat slot mercuric globe thwart
inward or xray :   go siluriformes
      under his sucking eye soldered
host words   he wasn't sure what
     he acted   seized
returning from awareness puncture
        a stable paradise, sealed.

the details at times are as vague as burn screams
if they hadn't droppt bombs
bone screams
if anyone actually likes Oxford St
groping, for one second totally blind
like ant sores
& that split is essential
drip drip drip, as if biting
& I'd put a razor to it
essential, is not vague
key word is Oxford St, is burn screams
as detailed as that, as vague, as clamped

silver burst
in pocket
jerk—

cash twist—

all the trees are
dead—

seven popstarz
scattered
in my coffee
drip
drip
shattered
on the palace
shot
big dog
big dog
all the trees
are bastards—

another cafe
skinned
three coins
drip
drip
drip—

spunk chrome
in old tin
prophets
grin

grin
three coins
big dog
all the trees
are shot
popstarz
scattered
in old tin
drip
on the palace
blade
big dog
on the palace
shattered
in old tin
cash burst
three coins
drip
drip
drip—

the words "we are loyal employees"
  were spoken on Tuesday's news
    in every doorway by tokens
bands of huddled mist,
              invisible,
    created from coins, small ones
and storms of teeth
          themselves being eaten
        in a block of solid rain, so that
    below your skin you would feel
the cells break
smeared
all kinds of dirty pix
with designs on your spine
as an economic diagram
recast as a roast flower
and forced into your fist, as a way of saying
                we love your
                loyalty
                your mouth, your
                erotic
                slot
                a fingernail in your glans
                a hand on your tongue
                can split &
          in the doorways petrol blistered
      shadows
            red wings
                  kill deer
                      thighs punched
                      in the system
                      for audit
                      brown stoking . . . .

I don't
for example
believe
that all you need is love
in a box
starred
disorders smile
in blue suit
expensive hair
honestly rearing
noises
false
they strap the pincer gloves
they kill you for no love
drag and believe
its stupid
glue keeps the face on
for 90 minutes
stamped
on the inverse side
rearing
coins drilled
palms outstretched
the click on the phone
is the thing in your throat
is echo level
at seizure rearing
shudder
the furnace is not in the post
the collective dream
is snapped price-tag
stamped
where I thought I had to have these

                                    noises
          & don't for example
believe that

86 him. He wasn't aware at this point just what battery acid could do. What does it mean, copyright in a landfill, encaged, magnetic. He was filmed looking manic on a suitably edgy street and was famous. At this stage it isn't clear if he has or hasn't loved. Should we name him. Mallard. Glebe. Twig. Music has been privatised, which means its everywhere, like sperm; split, sprayed and pointless like trying to fuck a window. The avant-garde is a gentrified zone, its address cash furnace. Pile it on him for several thousand units, run him like a lightbulb, his face in the magazines and his hands in considerable pain. Not just his glands, limit him. He can only count to 26 and then he starts to starve. Kiss this man. Glue him, show him everything. And keep the receipts.

'these' pictures have come in lately
                        under fingernails, behind
                  the eyes,
mingled with code in the hair
cracks in the genome where you can slip it in
                  and pump
anything, margarine in a fist

& why was 'Mr Blair' jerking
on Iraqi TV
            his front teeth voltaic
            if inserted in the slot
            the whole light will flicker
            he will still be 'that nameless substance'
            that guards are paid to watch after
                              'make no mistake'
the sky is not full of noise it is
the siren is not the point
                  is
these practices
of which a flag is capable and predicts
what happens to steel and glass and torn leather
when gravity, immense granite,
by which I mean the smiles of certain celebrities
            as if they were the weather itself
are attached, like barbed wire
was invented as a radical alternative to firelight,
just as NASA found a non-carbon life-form
            in folded light and blast box turning
            into those 'pictures' again
            actually intersected by them
which is what is meant by ghosts, or electricity
or a 'minister' looking upon these persons

as if they were cattle bodies twisted
                    burning
            penned in by . . . .

click
have a flower in your head
            is others scraping
      into burst geography
craven fingers click

glue, magnetized :

I don't want vinyl records
I want broken bone receptors—

fill in the form and leak it. we couldn't tell you if or not
we are radon clamps—
or sparks encrusted : what are your secret desires
wrapped in piano wire
found under one of the bridges—

hold on. does the traffic not worry
you <u>are</u>
no. a big gate at the end of the
no. what does
you.
talking.
to.   gas-lips.

Branson's mouth imposed
Branson's mouth imposed
Branson's mouth imposed
on

boil   <u>your stupid racist throat</u>

and he, who want to be adverts
have walked in off the map
inna
code : entryway to great big bag of pills
long green ones to
LICK IT

start here

this is a love poem in 42cm;
call that tattooed?
I say PRICE GUN

inburst of fast rip / like bee talk / razorswing

(bone sweat) give a fast name for radial enigma bursting the
neighbours. & I know what you mean about the verb 'to be' as
false name syndrome or those things that crawl on the leaves. the
key word in any diagram is 'to eat', my full name is partially we
glister, neutron stiff. he is closed like a beak is, hope is a
bourgeois word. bone is a living tissue which is a verb started as a
small mark. forgiveness is a bourgeois conceit so is hanging so is
blazing so

the city is noise reserves
split
acrylic bones
opened
five knuckle discount
fingered
          you're so . . . .

. . . . *lids flicker*

              sight crackle :
         the voice is ancient and
                   summons
     a pit of fist
         repeat playback
            inner bone rot
        field angelic whip crust
                 face replica. down
   in the cock circuit radio propels glister. shout
                   in curdled desire
     & again, broadcast bliss via
  rope and crane : dissected on a roadside
          for quick relief
      stitched
         numbered
            lash debates :
tune in, yell for help as a price sticker. let him speak
3   9   pause to reject and
          true muscles float
      on the stem
clamped in ghost meat. all the little popstars
         are happy, happy
     the perimeter loaded, forbidden boogie.

.... the map of London
is pure currency—
    cigarette holes
& bacon
    stains carefully
etched
face itch
forced
through the
eye, a
groin salt
    scattered
as torn glass:
the massed caves
        of Oxford St
memories over-rated
    hostage
stamp—
    why not
sell your skin,
last week's offer
        will wipe
    your stinging
face right off
if nothing is real
    means that cash is
        on full flow
        as the fire in Hoon's belly
    is a real furnace
& metals extend
even unto his mouth
is the hole in the window your hand
burst the sharp glints of light

                    in the viscous street
            voices
                    scorched
a noxious shiver of pure code
                    stuttering
spurting its temper off
                    the map itself

                        tongue rasp —
                        factor twitch —

        survive commerce on
     8   7
—*the solution?*
       no
but this is
    Cheapside splurge
         its alembic tin

[mailbox locked for
                      gas din : the sky
                             is a long line
                                  of noise
                             or maybe

settle. 9. be dust
and slice, receive
     wonder
   why do they love that
        ele-
                  mental face
          arranged like
      soap between thighs
          will flutter
               ceiling rip

the sky is clicks
hit remit

matter
matter

nothing of importance has ever been communicated by being gentle with a public: and this particular public, which has been so totally deprived of freedom and which has tolerated every sort of abuse, deserves less than any other to be treated gently.

(LICK IT —

Burnt Nickle (2004–2005)

. . . .morally
        certain whipchord
            assembles
            blank hydrocarbons
    for fist display
            your thigh
    parting
        arranged on
            the right side
        pass on
            my
                sweet
        ibuprofen
            to bitter
        ground self
            dumped
        in the fear flask
            a penny
                sharpened
            as salt
        ended
                in split rock
            the imaginary
            foam of those
    who would
                brand dream
        & sculpt
            the red disk
                threaded
            rock
        parted
    & chewed . . . . .

we understand
there is something divides
graphic charts
from monotheism
as an echo chamber
wherein
it is still the 1970s
in bleached form
inhabits the body
pump
on the fear floor
glamour
of twisted wire receptors
belief in identity
of proto-conglomerate
symbolism
trying to find a bin
to puke in
below ground

demand protection for sex dolls
as human
at pitch of bone relief
walking pronouns
as tender molecules
enlist the truth vow :
recuperate sex doll
position swallow
the pink stone
's fiscal body
twitch
enlist planets
as fricative rising plastic awareness
the morality arteries coil
inside your loyalty card
fried love
at the outset :
insurgents expected later.

social climbing among metals
        pits stereo
                transgressors
against refugees from the
                        pulse
        is a real splinter
    home for the alphabet
home of the smug
        compression : these people
are vulgar and
            cannot / will not
        use the correct trough
    are unavailable for use
                to lick
                out
    in his system the stars
are polished
                and creak melts
    of wax on their patents—
thumbs down
            for the grandees claim
a free film crew crushed
                    at the border.
    if the people won't speak
we can stitch their empty mouth
    the name of the game
is hog gruel, get that
                drilled in the palm
        of the earth's
        shrunken pit
held up as exemplary
                    city centre aflame
            and watched

by robots twitch
their message
                    will not be
        adhered, behind glass
we write the word
                    on our arms like little squirts
    collapsed
in the social cardiac day job

that the police station as system
has extended into the earth
and electric waves inoculate
visually it crackles
is internal / extends
tyramine palm arc
/ crack
in dirty protest
sponsored by the co-operative bank
is metic spark
is wasp cygnus
is under arrest
is the point not to ask who
but what are you

.... consumerism speaks only
in the products
it can clasp within its skin
is fenceproof
along the fault scale
eat what you are told and
when, what was
inevitable. star word claw
adjusted to bailiff cognition
dog-togs,
emblems of scenic hatred
from outside the position
try to keep it in your fist
is warm and giving
bacterial knowledge
as shudder, cardiac jism
as museum storage. shred it :
rampant codices
reinsert leopard print
the crowd in the shape of a triple x
squirting wire technique
grinding echo spit
to dot squirt
to ivy compressed
mouth
the juice ditch
your tongue
at the perimeter where the town folds
cop — disc
reeled in
at entrance to the public mouth frozen
&
unlived socialism woken

by a knock on bailiff script,
pledge to chew lip
for only five decades :

on cell wall
cygnus
interruptus
you
will stay here
stamped
for five years
into whip-
chord semblance
crouch
inside gravity
field
ejaculate
the furnace =
2   3
on the blast
organ
do not suck
do not use tooth
oscillators
repair image
of owls eating London
in slow motion circuit awareness
clamps halogen faders arranged on the tube plan
nostalgia triggered by human dust
I'm a human
fly
I say buzz buzz buzz

Verdict :

beg neighbour : as a piss-squeal we are pathetic too
& would invent a big cannon
in the spot post-office was
a rivet, glowing.
pause. the room
is zone exclusion open
at the brown river impact :
pretty ones pressed into rock formation. tiny as plugged follicles
sound better scratched
tampered info
policy screw
brown wet stuff. & photographed. the bottom corner
is now a colonel
flying / simmer four hours
& lick all over clock pattern
internal
raindrops
crack
pane
until its made legal & injected
slow & nasty
as the sky is
leaking
radio stutters till J-lo =
Brixton
resort /
beg spectacle. thread chrome torque scrape. the rivet was scrape
denied surgery for reasons of ugly
fire in the heads of
think. is possible.
ugliness tightened
till statue falls
the footfall on
they all had a big job to do. he was a big job. took eight feet under rib-cage

scalpels. got him. stamp screw coupons. body landfill =
£20 worth
vision market +
rigged arthopods = rock formation.
but what he expects is. rigged. as a neural function
is best poisoned
spine separates into (1) what we were told to know &
(2) what is closed into its job-ditch is a steel gag. beg
now. no throat to speak of or clarify social climbing
as disappointment registered so (3) stone = camera.
do not project it on metal. it is possible to discover
any person in any part of the world / when hidden /
when alive & dead.

Oona King

halt. if you say
like maybe destroy rock
   n roll is pointless
like the feudal system
     & as relevant : halt.
        you live there, as in
        index = last month's interior
        rock n roll gets defensive
        panic juice replayed
as if to say gas. as if
           resistor circuits encode
           tongue archive. get it
           there, eat it, is
           tithe collapse
           frequency
        as if. halt. if you say
here's some things to do with metal wire
here's some things to do : reclaim dereliction. in the centre
                vortex simulation reset
                science as
      flood archive = service industry
            with tiny stimulant structures
            busk isolation as strum ideas
            inside capital's head moving
            without severed letters speak
            his masters voice includes
            past time gone to the wall
      as if interior echoes circuit
            where the hand is placed dialectically
                damaged by fingernails screech
                    what solid bone wants
     is not to be left alone = memory guards as if halt
                  each celebrities potential

                    for deterioration breaks
                       circuit shrinks
                  granite density
             as voice opens
             or if you say
        what destroy rock n roll
        would even mean at genital level
        broken / a vote for freedom / broken on cobbled /
                       siege bubbles
        & just as quickly televised, pleasuring its own transgression
      as if anything could be as boring. strapped down. poor fucker.
    consider the marxist tradition as chloroform gash. halt. be surprised. say bang.
  ask what flicker = bang. repeat bang. consider the imperialism of frozen bellies
        shipped into all mouths REPEAT as if music
                  was this useless.
  feedback has entered the word 'bibliography'
        tunnelled into airplay disturbed
        by the nightwatch is what is said
             licking cum off his own face
                  is cash buzz stops his itching fist
  falls. nothing falls. abrupt flash wipes radio
                  wrapped in wire strings
                  inside his mouth a meat
                            war
                  rolls out the entertainment
                  as if last year's static
                  could really clean the circuit
                  follows like a bus into
                  what the map conceals
                  is this hand :
                  its twist & squeak. halt.
  it seems that now they've all got the same head
  talks up a threat prepared earlier
  from the letter cast

nailed behind the eyes. entertainment is your talk.
you like to keep it at entry level
& why not. eat. raise dense matter centres
as string vibration
break window

with your elders = what stars mean
when kept between the cheeks
the pulse reopens subterranean rings
like rock n roll considered as scenery—
brownfield contamination
plant homeless. London has moved on. the whipping posts
are expensive. plant homeless.
panic as they start to speak and
breathe event. insert liability cards down left ear flick penile derangement as
monitor, as standard.
those who have exited molecular level
are passed off as a universe fit to live in
speaker cones :
the dense black clouds that appear at tide, that
drop down

one by one. shout it out
on expense account
scratch the song into his own fingers
as if braille style
sprayed a trust circuit
over blatant surgical toss. but can it matter what guitars will say
when what we ie everyone can eat
is solid
squeal
as if convinced the circuit cursed. the ghosts of sums of money
wailing by
necessity.

~

you know that 86% of Londoners
       think cool is brand heated interiors. tell em its so.
       tip the right shirt down your
      throat enters helium dust that from your lip
           spark
        riot now /
but the answer is what you listen

      you don't
    tell them say what you
   understand as circuit breakers as
          understanding
     is minimum
  level
 entry.

Document (2005)

Filter OD

speaking in a language whose strange melody might not belong on Earth. . . .

David Nicol is in jail
endurance as nerve end. photon
screw. photography of dead people
sealed with letters. you want
atom. is a nail, says
amygdala, finger in the earth,
that means wake up now.
this is the ever same
as abject ghost buzz shatter
you in voice prism; adjust
you, says, countersign / fixion, says
star kick equal not you
twitch radio in burnt red,
your juncture voice implode. starling.
scratch while your pennies sleep,
say dial, where the wiring
ends in what you think.
pass cable street as thorn
toss, or do not eat
this meat this glass, displaced
o useless head. cross street.
sly gland occupation. heritage agitation
as muscle spurt. name yourself.
this is hare spree. eat
your sympathy, is product, arouse
its role in human life :

invent permission. take it off.
you feel good as itch
star is ancient suck is
fixed. rust is fear circuit.

rust is next big thing
like shoes. you like shoes.
jazz is nice. like it
nice at five speed arousal.
limit it. then imagine celebrities
had to duck sniper rimshot
at every burst rhythm cluster
is unacceptable. now you withdraw
or wake up and yell
those are not (are not)
my beautiful hands. love it.
or everything we know assembles
in magazine insertion. you are.
are not your beautiful face
to fill you with vocabulary
jazz is sleep. prefer servitude.
or our gated community smiles
as social horizon. pit flame.
march on Whitehall. suck vortex.
or fuck it, you lied,
say 45 minutes, say broadcast
cell whip and foam lick :
the single psychotic individual sleeps
on string—is not you
are blank within these institutions.
say thorn. the starry mess.
say buzz. say eat it
don't exist outside your mouth,
say fire is further networks
of snatch angels. rictus placement
at office level radon buzz
as voice strobe will enter
nine to five lymph system

saturation as buzz circuit. private.
the disappeared want to know
what rich people won't understand :
Cable St is fright filter,
is vacant, is irritation. or
reach implosive necessity (not me)
scattered like a bad debt.
see that ladybird. eat it.
level P would like to
keep memory of it short
like that of the world
is more interesting than you
should buy some of this.
client. please. that voices surround
and grip stories between levels
you had locked. client hand.
you had burned them. names
equal clients. the power off.
flicker them, or say spark.
flower glue. say cyst or
memory. count it. and divide
what always was level P
which does not mean pandemonium
far from it, black dot
as coin resort. now swim.
now slot in—fire, make
client now from blast rock.
replay kitsch as social option
or pretend cable st is
nice. say nice. say boil
in check-out queue, be plastic
hour spent tonguing strangers
in other people's hair. or

rub it, then it buzz,
on echo. say buzz slot.
say spit. say why you
fucked till dawn then hands
broke. music. broke. music. broke
work of the five senses.
gather them, fix them; use
as gathering of memory scatter
next week : LONDON FALLS. borrowed.
forget it. had locked them,
rat seal (open) music fade
static is what you said
open mouth. coin. say coin.
take any tower say statue
as particle suspended in oil
receptor fixion. the monument network.
if doesn't fit its true.
walk catacomb as fear circuit.
no city of the sun
to interpret the prime minister
as (a) nail, (b) priest,
(c) decent venereal distance. whatever.
the first circle is impenetrable.
admit these. silo, blake, urizen.
laugh now. insert learned fear.
the fourth circle is throat
bush. head down. sick sick.
the second circle is you
puke muscle thatch and jizz
is nice. no nice. fix.
in the arena of heads
nerve flash & buzz memory
in the sixth circle method

is hunger is easy money.
but never use these words,
understand that you are medicine
and very easy to starve.
say this : your love is
the point where it blisters.
in the third circle say
walk on these things only,
say snob say volt pith
the fifth circle was cancelled.
eat service. eat romance. envy.
never say envy, music, envy.
the seventh circle is obvious
reports say black dot. invade.
but the hours say territory,
say surgeons fixed on body
break open what is clear:
parade flesh as snob vortex
reverse the current or, humiliated,
go home. sing. is nice.
say this. you prefer servitude.
lets be nice. hurt me.
now forget. file and forget
or mumble some numb crap
included like a machine is
filed away in half of
one of your english hours
don't want to be pressed
inside each day of jagged
ease is a universe with
closing sale now breaking down.

Document

and soon asylum seekers will
sit in spit in box;
no land to speak of,
as all cities are curdled,
spat through algebraic memory, oblique
and polite. fatwa on numbers
who walk in greater circles,
but cities require danger as
all else is too smooth
like a faked baby neutralised
with nails : Branson as interpreter.
Richard Branson as mass memory.
Richard as mouth that says
run it like a firm
is no distortion, job seekers
recognise the friendly bacteria as
they do not wear ties
and grin in unison in
high alert, wear chemical suits
and join hands to keep
us out, sick bells. competition
is simple : get the best
seekers find the hidden seroxat
under black stones, botox stubble.
insert transients in cellular matter.
insert into property prices a
green dye, watch its progress—
vascular level—roast with garlic,
toss northern terraces to damp
sand, control information and grind
their stones and scatter the
value of land multiplies as
rumours of heritage coagulate like

sucking clams. look, a picture.
put a gate on it.
breathe in good film dust.
interpret the A–Z, any city
as satellite pincer movement, the
implications are that barren. we
recommend hibernation as first investment :
rich people are growing on
shredded voices gather gas underground
& Branson says make adventure
was meant to be great
but well is kinda dull
frames in specific parameters. eat
nice gas, nice exterior, nice
mass memory with running electricity.
the commune an aching sore:
we are all on pills
and torture. we'll take anything.

Document: No Admittance

no admittance to
glass shift
from behind flat
static / glacial
radio enclosed
& ignite
the very young will tell you
it landed way back
before official memory
like 1980 or something
is marked
understand its privacy:
the camera has rights
to make you
extracted from
each time your life
is playback
as a series of boxes
your frame
grinds
till pleasure is
baked joy of department glass, the
house rattles or
last night I dreamt I was
on the tube
and when I was I woke
in consultation: this advice
given to the very young:
pour aerosol, mark it,
imagine London flutter
its tight hand
inscript it, make
big groan, split

                private: give feedback on
            what it means
                to be inside this
                    sealed, in
                        wax rows
                like being patronised
            one day on the Strand
        told me heat planet,
                    gas ignition, very likely
                        so why finish
                    anything
                words tangle: hurtle
            boulder constellation
                of planet gas & celestial spurt
        to mark the privacy boundary
    "no admittance except on business"
                        for broadcast
                    magnetic scrub & hermetic ion
            from A-Z turned
                        inside out:
                some light gone
            for the territory
    means switch em off.

Document: Suicide Note

London the movie is
            "get out"
    "we all"
        "should stop lying"—

the prime minister would like
us not to understand, has
closed doors that any child
would and
        or shift: the
      the position, is
     it goes like this, you walk in
       take your face
           off, plug in
           identity as permafrost
           is flyspray.
           is. is. is
           easy, you go back home
           sleep your skeleton
           out. ride him. his shift crust.
           ride him and
           stop.
               get off at Aldgate
           smash Stonehenge
and queue up inside
what tourists want
at capex capacity
        the dull lager of our fear: tenants extra
             as interpretation
        the prime minister would like us
to say why. say don't know
but come on, the idea is simple
         like Digby Jones / his mouth available

                    in various sizes
                            insert gradients
                    in the social
                            stitch a loan trickle:
                    you learn to love them, tectonic
                    as / I see you baby
                    are composed
            of mission plans and shaking
                    your—forty quid for a capex shot
                            as   silence imposed
on London is hard spit
conveniently lost in discussion
of business innovation group
or BIG for short:
            have you got a BIG idea?
            when you submit an ideal
            to BIG it goes through
            an innovation funnel-
like lock the library. we are all in storage & all the time
                            as icon dust, siren lash:
whatever. "I feel beautiful tonight"
                    as cartoon noise
                    photocopied
to secure funds and
houses made of pure chemicals only:

there are reasons to
don't say don't run—
unload it. loot the supermarket.

Printed in the United Kingdom
by Lightning Source UK Ltd.
106527UKS00001B/97-102